JOHN PATRICK BOUTILIER

ARDUS PUBLICATIONS

ALSO AVAILABLE FROM ARDUS PUBLICATIONS

Available on the createspace.com eStore and amazon in 6" x 9" paperback, and on amazon in kindle format:

REFLECTIONS, John Patrick Boutilier, 2016.

WHAT MANNER OF MADNESS, John Patrick Boutilier, 2015.

PHOTOGRAPHS AND MEMORIES, John Patrick Boutilier, 2015.

VISIONS OF BLUE, John Patrick Boutilier, 2015.

THE CLOVER IN THE GARDEN, John Patrick Boutilier, 2015.

A DIVINE MADNESS: AN ANTHOLOGY OF MODERN LOVE POETRY VOLUMES 1 6, John Patrick Boutilier and Gina Ancheta Agsaulio, 2015.

VOICES OF HUMANITY, VOLUMES 1 3, John Patrick Boutilier and Gina Ancheta Agsaulio, 2016.

ARDUS PUBLICATION'S 2015 CHRISTMAS ANTHOLOGY, John Patrick Boutilier and Gina Ancheta Agsaulio, 2015.

A BOUQUET OF VERSE VOLUMES 1 and 2, John Patrick Boutilier and Gina Ancheta Agsaulio, 2016.

THE ANGELIC HEART, Gina Ancheta Agsaulio, 2015.

THE ENCHANTED SEA, Gina Ancheta Agsaulio, 2015.

CELESTIAL THOUGHTS, Gina Ancheta Agsaulio, 2015.

FRAGRANCE OF A WILD ROSE, Gina Ancheta Agsaulio, 2015.

DARK TALES: 5 TALES OF TERROR, Joyce Ann Marie Gage, 2015.

ONCE UPON A DREAM, Joyce Ann Marie Gage, 2015.

POCKET FULL OF POETRY, Joyce Ann Marie Gage, 2016.

IMMORTAL HEARTS: DARK SIDE OF THE MOON, Jacqueline Gallant, 2016.

A SYMPHONY IN WORDS, Michael Brent Startup, 2015.

NAKED

John Patrick Boutilier

ARDUS PUBLICATIONS
2017

© 2017 JOHN PATRICK BOUTILIER

Check out ARDUS Publications on Facebook:

https://www.facebook.com/ardus.publications

First Printing: 2017

ISBN- 13: 978-1542534802

ISBN-10: 1542534801

ARDUS PUBLICATIONS
Courtenay, British Columbia, Canada

DEDICATION

To all lovers and those who desire peace.

ABOUT THE AUTHOR

John was born in Port Morien, Nova Scotia, Canada. When he was 20 years old, he left his home and joined Princess Patricia's Canadian Light Infantry, 3rd Battalion. While in the military, John married and, with his wife, had 3 children, Patrick, Krystal and Ester. Upon leaving the military, John went back to school and earned a Bachelor of Science (with Honours) and Master of Science degree in psychology from the University of Victoria, Victoria, British Columbia, Canada. He had also completed his comprehensive examinations and stopped there, with only his dissertation remaining.

John began writing poetry and lyrics when he was only 15 years old and, though there have been long spells where he's written little or nothing, he continues to write to this day.

John's poetry and lyrics have traditionally centered on matters of the heart but his writings are evermore being focused on important sociopolitical issues.

John Patrick Boutilier

ABOUT THIS BOOK

This book is basically divided into two parts. The first half is devoted to the topic of love: its desires, its gain and its loss. The second half is a mix of sociopolitical, inspirational and general poetry.

The book is called NAKED because the poems are expressions of my naked soul.

TABLE OF CONTENTS

AM I NAKED

Am I naked
I am when I speak with you
For every word that we share
Betrays my thoughts most true

When I tell you how I feel
Be I happy or be I sad
That's exactly where I am
Feel you it good or bad

There are at most but a few
With whom I share my soul
But I do with you quite willingly
Because in you I know

You will love me despite my errs
As you have shown throughout the years

ARE YOU NAKED

Are you naked
Is what I'm seeing real
Are the things you're telling me
Really what you feel

You tell me that you love me
But do you love me true
Or do you only say the words
Because you know how I love you

Play not games with my heart
For past love has left it weak
I've had enough of superficial
It is true love that I seek

If you agree not treat me wrong
I will love you my life long

ARE WE NAKED

Are we naked
Are we ready to believe
Each and every one of us
Must learn to perceive

But to perceive the truth for some
Can be a painful thing
Even where the truth of love
Is offered in a ring

Explain to me your reason
Why you chose to run away
And tell me true why you've returned
Seeking my love today

You claim you've learned you love me true
Never once have I doubted my love for you

ARE THEY NAKED

Are they naked
Or are they clothed in lies
Is that their true face we see
Or is that but disguise

Some of those who call us friend
Who come to our table and feed
Can we be sure they'll stand by us
In our times of need

Many seem to come with want
And we are willing to share
But if the table was reversed
Would their friendship still be there

Sometimes 'tis better to be poor
To know your friends are friends for sure

SOMETIMES WE NEED SOMEONE

Sometimes we need someone to listen, not someone to speak
To hear what we have to say, all the thoughts we think
We don't need their opinions, just a caring ear
To release our many burdens, to release our many fears

Sometimes we need someone, someone just to offer us a smile
To give us just a moment, that we might breathe for a while
Someone that can show us there will be a brighter day
Someone who by listening alone can take our pain away

I hope I've been that someone and I know that if need be
You will be that someone, that someone there for me
I hope you know by now, my friend, I'm always by your side
And I will always be there, however we are tried

My ear is always yours, my friend, to listen to your woes
To listen to your complaints, wherever your thoughts go
I will always be there for you, right until the end
If all the world departs you, know alone I'll be your friend

WHAT IS IT I WOULD DO IF YOU EVER LEFT ME

You ask me what it is I would do
If you ever left me
I hope we never find out
I believe if I ever lost you
I think I'd cease to be
Of that I've no doubt

How could I go on
Without you, all life's meaning is gone
You're so essential to me
Without you, I'm not sure I could be

I know you know it's true
You're the only one
The only one for me
I'm so in love with you
But we've just begun
We've got eternity

How could I get by
Without you, why would I even try
You're every beat of my heart
Without you, I'd be torn apart

I know I've said it before
But I'll say it now
I need your love
There's nothing I need more
You're my why and how
All I ever dream of

If you ever left me girl
I'd feel lost
I'd feel tossed
If you ever break my heart
I'd be down for a while
But I'd rise and I'd smile
I'd go the extra mile
I'd strut and I'd style
To be
To be without you with me

How could I survive
Without you, I'd still be alive
I'd take my broken heart
Without you, I'd make a new start

I know I'd feel the pain
For a very long time
Because I love you
But I would try again
From despair I'd climb
Seeking love anew

You ask me what it is I would do
If you ever left me
I hope we never find out
I believe if I ever lost you
I would continue to be
Of that I've no doubt

BE MY VALENTINE

Be my valentine
Give me your lovin' and I'll give you mine
My mind is set on you
No other woman could ever do

I hope you understand
I'm trying to win your hand
Give you everything
Like a diamond ring
And a wedding band

I knew when we met
You I had to get
Your sweet perfume
It filled the room
I can smell it yet

Be my valentine
You're better than perfect you are divine
I hurt without you
You've no idea what I'm going through

I've been so alone
Livin' life on my own
If I may be bold
I need you to hold
I wanna make you moan

I wanna know your kiss
I wanna know your bliss
I wanna hold you tight
Each and every night
Not a moment miss

Be my valentine
You got the power make my life shine
My heart I give to you
Know that it's fragile and know that it's true

Give me your answer please
You got me on my knees
Say you'll be mine
You'll be my valentine
And please don't tease

Be my valentine
You're hotter than lava and sweeter than wine
My love is meant for you
None have made me feel the way you do

Be my valentine
Give me your lovin' and I'll give you mine
My mind is set on you
No other woman could ever do

DREAM OF ME AND I WILL DREAM OF YOU

Dream of me and I will dream of you
Together in sleep we'll be as one
All that we'd wish while we were awake
In our dreams they can be done

Laugh and cry, joke and sigh
But in every word reveal
The innermost secrets of ourselves
That from others we conceal

For sharing is most intimate
When sharing of the soul
And when it's done with the right one
Revealing has no toll

We have seen each other true
There's nothing left to hide
So in our dreams at night we share
What we cannot keep inside

WHAT YOU NEED

What your lips need most are my lips
Embraced in passion's kiss
A moment oft we've dreamed of
Where delivered what we miss

What your ears need most are my words
To tell you of my love
While I hold you in my arms
Manifest what spoken of

What your heart needs most is my heart
A heart that's pure and true
A heart that's freely given
A heart that's but for you

What you need is me, my dear
And when you're ready, I'll be here

WHAT IS A WOMAN

She is the dawn
She is the spring
She is the harvest
She is everything

She is the breath
She is the love
She is the hope
She is the dove

She is the glue
She is the soul
She is the heart
She is the whole

She is the mother
She is the friend
She is the beginning
She is the end

YOU ARE

You are so sexy
You are so sweet
I can't wait until the day we meet
Oh the pleasure
Oh the bliss
Oh the magic when we first kiss

You are my dream
You're my fantasy
You're absolutely everything to me
You are the why
You are the how
You're exactly what I need right now

I love everything about you
Everything you say and do
You're my dream come true
Let me make this clear
I desire you here
Forever be near

You are so pretty
You are so smart
You came along and won my heart
I was impressed
I was amazed
No one ever have I so praised

You're my best friend
You're my deepest desire
You're the one I most admire
You are the goal
You are the prize

You're the only woman I idolize

I love how you're always caring
Always giving, always sharing
But when needed fierce and daring
I've never known a heart so pure
Such strength in someone so demure
So childlike yet so mature

YOU ARE THE ONE

You are the one
The one I love
The one most dear
You are the sun

You are the stars
You are the sky
You are the reason
You are the why

You are the answer
You are the question
You are the beginning
You are the destination

You are the one
The one I love
The one most dear
You are the sun

COME THEN

In answer to what you have stated
Know what you desire I can meet
And if you're sure you're strong enough
Come then and feel the heat

Come then and be pleasured
Come then and know the bliss
Come then and feel the passion
Come then and know my kiss

Be my lover
Be my friend
Be my beginning
Be my end

Feel my love
Feel my lust
Feel my want
Feel my must

Come then and be my lover
Come then and be mine
Come then and be forever
Come then and be divine

You've asked and you shall receive
If what you want is wanted true
You can possess all you desire
The choice, my Dear, is up to you

Come then I am waiting
Come then to my embrace
Come then to know what true love is
Come then us face to face

THE RELIGION OF LOVE

Let us start a new religion
We will call it love
And let us give it all the best
The others failed of

All who want will be accepted
If they want to be
We will accept no division
No differences will we see

Love knows no colour
Love knows no race
Love knows no status
Love knows no place

We will have a single goal
Unity for all
But you will have the freedom
To avoid our call

We will offer you respect
Because we love you true
We will welcome you with open arms
If come to us you do

Love is compassion
Love is providing care
Love is doing right
Love is being fair

We will seek to help the needy
We will provide for the poor
We will see that the human race
Becomes more than ever before

If I were to choose a path
Love would be the one for me
And if I were to offer answer
Love would the answer be

Love is the answer
Love is the right
Love is the way
Love is the light

A BROKEN HEART IS NEVER TRULY HEALED

A broken heart is never truly healed
It is merely mended
Its most important functions absent
From the pain they seem suspended

The person continues to go on
They exist and they work
They suffer insult and they suffer pain
Without as much as flinch or jerk

Often taken advantage of
In their weakened state
The injured seem to accept abuse
As if it were their fate

I urge them rise above their pain
Rise above self-hate and doubt
Rise above their coward masters
Rise above and cast them out

A broken heart is never truly healed
But it can be repossessed
Take back that which belongs to you
Let your freedom be expressed

Make yourselves free today
Free to find one loves you true
At least please free yourselves, my dears
From the hate you feel for you

FROM YOUR TENDER WORDS

It is from your tender words
I retain some hope
It is but from your presence here
I continue cope

It is but from your smile
I can see the light of day
It is but from your love for me
I've not yet faded away

It is but from your strength
I am able continue on
It is but from your faith in me
I know will come the dawn

It is from fact that you are
That I am able be
It is from fact that without you
I doubt there'd be a me

IT IS BY YOUR DEEDS

It is by your deeds I judge you
It is by your deeds I define you
It is by your deeds that I decide
If I want you by my side

It is by your deeds you show
It is by your deeds I know
It is by your deeds that I see
If I want you part of me

It is by your deeds you express
It is by your deeds you impress
It is by your deeds you win my love
If ever my love was wanted of

It is by your deeds you will graded
It is by your deeds I'll be persuaded

WHEN I AM HEADING OFF TO BED

When I am heading off to bed
So in need of my sleep
If you feel the want at all
You're welcomed in my bed come creep

Know my desire will be hard
For my want is truly strong
And if we begin may I assure
I will be wanting all night long

And finally when you awake
After being ravished so
We can begin again if you wish
Let love and passion grow

My love is something I can't hide
My passion you feel deep inside

MY BABY LIKES TO WALK IN THE RAIN

My Baby likes to walk in the rain
So we walk along
Singing a song
Some friends think we are insane
But we always have fun
With or without the sun

My Baby loves to hold my hand
I know she loves me so
She never lets it go
Only those in love understand
We love each other so much
We always have to touch

Put your hand in mine
Let's walk in the rain
I don't care if the world
Thinks us both insane
I'll do anything
You want me to do
All that matters to me
Is my love for you

My Baby likes to walk in the rain
She even adores
When the rain pours
And though I'd prefer to abstain
A simple caress
Assures her a yes

Put your hand in mine
Let's walk in the rain
I don't care if the world

Thinks us both insane
I'll do anything
You want me to do
All that matters to me
Is my love for you

My Baby likes to walk in the snow
As the snowflakes fall
One and all
And in her eyes and smile I know
I feel inside
I belong by her side

NINI

Thank you, Dear Nini
Goddess divine
My only complaint
Is you are not mine

Now if you were mine
What would we do
I would not care
As long as with you

Would we hike a mountain
What trail would we tread
Would we watch a sad movie
Would we even leave bed

If you were more bright
The sun would shy away
If you offered more light
We would know but the day

Thank you, Dear Nini
Always in my heart
As long as you are
True love you impart

MY DEAREST GINA

You are so beautiful
Words cannot convey
And you grow more beautiful
Each and every day

Your smile ever warms my heart
Your words enlighten my mind
Your influence so obvious
'Tis apparent to the blind

For a lady such as you
A man would dare any task
There is no deed he would not do
If you were but to ask

'Tis easier for me than most
To say the things I say
For of my love I'm proud to boast
And it grows with every day

WANG BING

How can I describe you
Do such words even exist
How am I a mortal man
Portray what angels can't resist

I can only say in simple terms
The wonder that I see
And there are none in this world
Can compare to thee

I wonder how it would feel
To know your tender kiss
I expect in your embrace
I would come to know true bliss

I wish I were a better man
For I am no way worthy you
But then I doubt that any are
I doubt most gods would do

I wonder how it would feel
To stroke your skin so soft
To have my hand upon your leg
A fantasy thought oft

I wish I were a richer man
That I could give you what you're due
But I am but a poet poor
And in no way am worthy you

SHE CAME BY WITH SOME GUY, GRABBED SOMETHING AND WAS GONE

She came by with some guy
Grabbed something and was gone
She came by with some guy
Grabbed something and moved on
There's nothing more to say
I haven't seen her since that day
She came by with some guy
Grabbed something and was gone

I never tried to look for her
Why should I even care
She never said a word to me
The last time she was here
I was standing in the kitchen
Makin' myself a cup of tea
When she came bursting through the door
And didn't even look at me

She came by with some guy
Grabbed something and was gone
She came by with some guy
Grabbed something and moved on
There's nothing more to do
Apparently we're through
She came by with some guy
Grabbed something and was gone

I wasn't sure what she took
But I knew something was gone
My best guess was she took something
She and the guy could pawn

I suppose the fault was mine
For daring to play the game
But since that day she went away
I've never been the same

She came by with some guy
And because I love her so
When she came by with some guy
I just let her go
She came by with some guy
And though it seems absurd
When she came by with some guy
She didn't say a word

She came by with some guy
Grabbed something and was gone
She came by with some guy
Grabbed something and moved on
I wish she'd told me why
Or at least had said goodbye
She came by with some guy
Grabbed something and was gone

I took some time to realize
What it was she took that day
But now I know exactly what
It was she took away
She left behind her diamond ring
The day she did depart
The only thing I found missing
Was she who'd won my heart

She came by with some guy
Grabbed something and was gone
She came by with some guy
Grabbed something and moved on

The day she did depart
I lost she who'd won my heart
She came by with some guy
Grabbed something and was gone

She came by with some guy
She'd chosen over me
When she came by with some guy
I decided set her free
She came by with some guy
I watched them drive away
Since she came by with some guy
I've missed her everyday

COME AND CUDDLE

Come and cuddle now my dear
Come and cuddle now sincere
Come and cuddle say I love you
Come and cuddle hear I love you too

Come and cuddle with me tonight
Come and cuddle hold me tight
Come and cuddle show me true
Come and cuddle the love in you

Come and cuddle let me feel
Come and cuddle know your love real
Come and cuddle throughout the night
Come and cuddle your pure delight

Come and cuddle with me my dear
Come and cuddle ever near

I BELIEVE IN YOU

I have loved
I have lost
I've known the pleasure
I've known the cost
I have felt the warmth
Of loves true embrace
I have felt the cold
When it's loss I had face
I've been the fool
Who gave all his heart
Only to be abused
My heart torn apart
One might think I'd abandon
The idea of love that's true
But I know you are out there somewhere
And I believe in you

ONE LAST DEED

If I were to die this moment
But offered one last deed to do
The only deed I'd want engage
Is one last kiss with you
If I'd one last thing to do
I'd share a kiss with you

If I were offered one last vision
Before my life expire
I would wish to see our love
Before me unfold entire
With she I most desire
With she who gave life fire

I have always loved you true
And even death it will not end
I will wait on other side
Till to me the angels choose you send
You are my love and my best friend
May our union never end

I pray you feel as I feel
I pray you love me too
That we may forever be together
As I imagine true lovers do
I want show my love is true
Throughout eternity with you

WHAT DO I SEE WHEN I LOOK AT THEE

What do I see when I look at thee
I see the reason, I know the why
For all that exists on earth, in sky
That is what I see when I look at ye

'Tis with great zeal I explain how I feel
This love so great I feel for you
This love so pure, this love so true
This love so real for my ideal

Perhaps one day, one day some way
You'll know what I see before my eyes
You'll understand my love, its size
How I pray soon comes that day

Then I ponder, when my love's depth you see
Might you finally commit then your heart to me

THE MOST DIFFICULT THING

The most difficult thing in life is loving someone so pure
So deep and so true
But they don't love you
What do you do

And they say all the words that you want to hear
Their words insincere
Though you desire them dear
And so want them be true

It can be so hard to say no
So hard to let go
To admit that you know
She'll never love you

When you die inside
When you've cried and cried
When you've tried and tried
What else can you do

No reason rejoice
But by your own choice
You continue give voice
That you desire

Without love what is life
But endless strife
Loneliness rife
More fuel for the pyre

A BITTER PILL

If you cannot scream to the world you love someone,
You don't love them
If they cannot scream to the world they love you,
They don't love you

© John Patrick Boutilier, 2017, All Rights Reserved.

HOW I MISS THOSE LIPS

How I miss those tender lips
Your kiss evermore sweet
My hands upon your shapely hips
How still my heart skips beat

To hold you in my arms forever
To always know your fire
To be without your presence never
Is my great desire

Come and share with me your smile
Shine its brilliant light on me
Be my lover for a while
That while eternity

My hand awaits your hand to hold
The world awaits our story told

COME AND WRAP YOUR LEGS AROUND ME

Come and wrap your legs around me
I desire be deep inside
Let me give you the love I've been hiding
But can no longer hide
Let me taste your pleasure
As you climax to my kiss
Let us give each other all the joy
That both of us so miss
I know how much you want me
Nowhere as much as I need you
I know that together you and I
There is nothing we can't do
Take my kiss and know the bliss
That in its absence we'd both miss
Take my kiss and please know this
Without you there is but abyss

SAY YES MY LOVE

Say yes my love
I tire of sleeping alone
I hug my pillow but it does not satisfy
I need someone to call my own

One kiss
As long as I draw breath
May our lips never part
At least until my death

Your skin against mine
Your touch heals me
I feel complete only in your arms
As if we're meant to be

Alone is being without you
Without the presence of your light
Without you there's but darkness
Me wandering in the night

I love you
Could you possibly love me
I truly am a good man
Give me chance and you will see

CONFESSIONS OF A LONELY HEART

I know you are out there
Perhaps seeking me as I seek you
She who wants to share an epic love
She who seeks the life I do

I reach out my arms
Trying to find you in the darkness
There are cold things trying to entangle me
Seeking upon my soul caress

The Cold, they lie and say they love me
But I sense their motive
They seek to torture, to cause me pain
'Tis by such actions alone they live

I know you are out there
She who wants the life I do
She who wants me epic love
I can sense she seeks me too

I've taken comfort in the Cold
Though I know it be a liar
Another betrayer of the heart
Not the she I desire

Loneliness too often
It can weaken the strongest wall
There are times when even a freezing touch
Is better than no touch at all

I know you are out there
Somewhere in the abyss
Sometimes allowing yourself to be deceived

To ease the loneliness

Despite the myriad falsities
However abundant they may be
We must remember we exist
We are not a fantasy

I believe we'll find each other
Though I know not where or when
One day our dream, it will come true
I feel it deep within

And I believe in love
I believe in the impossible
I believe in the heart
I believe in you

I know you are out there
Seeking me as I seek you
She who wants to share an epic love
She who seeks the life I do

OH BUT TO KISS YOUR LIPS SO SWEET

Oh but to kiss your lips so sweet
To know the taste on day we meet
The lips, the hips I long caress
The body I desire undress

Your breasts so perk, your form so tight
Oh how I wish I held you tonight
Your perfect body with mine entwined
In us passion will be defined

Your face is beauty by definition
And so inspires my admission
And my admission is but to say
I love you more with every day

I pray forever days never cease
That my love for you may but increase

FOR NO ONE DEEPER

For no one deeper in love could fall
Than for she, the most desired of all
More than any woman ever known
More than any beauty ever shown

There are none more sweet of heart than she
None more loving could ever be
If I were to have but single wish
I would wish least once to know her kiss

A million kisses everyday
Would not even begin allay
The desire that I feel for her
For such she causes my passions stir

And if one day God's will be done
Her heart and mine will beat as one

THE MORNING KISS

Is it the morning kiss
That keeps a smile upon her face
The kiss I awaken her with
As I take her in embrace
Her smile as I hold her near
Speaks more than ears could ever hear

There is something in her touch
A feeling I cannot explain
I can only say this true
Without her touch there is but pain
A pain without her knows no rest
A pain I feel deep within my chest

I demonstrate my love for her
In everything I do
It seems a million times a day
I tell her, "I love you"
But every day it begins with this
A tender embrace and the morning kiss

THE TRUTH IS HARDER

The truth is harder
Than a thousand lies to tell
Truth wins in the end
Even where truth causes pain
A lie leaves nothing to gain

There's times we want believe lies
Accept falsehoods blind can see
We abandon truth
We give to wants and desires
To source of our fires

The fire that burns in me is want of you
From the moment I first saw you I loved you true
It is a fire that burns ever hot
Though it seems for me your fire is aught

I KNOW LONELINESS

I know loneliness
I have been empty for years
A shell with no soul
Someone ever wanting you
Someone wanting love you true

There were times I thought you found
Only to learn I was wrong
Ever the dreamer
I held the hope you were real
My loneliness heal

But I remain empty as ever I was
Still seeking the one who'll complete me
I'll keep on searching if only because
In a dream I was promised we'd be

YOU ARE WHY

You are why life exists my dear
And I exist but to hold you near
To admire the perfection that is thee
To admire the vision that I see

Do I have the words to convey
To say everything I need to say
Ten thousand books and ten thousand more
Are not enough my words to store

How can I describe a beauty such as thee
When no words come close to describing ye
Perfect even seems such lame description
When it comes to your depiction

You are the one, the epitome
There's no other could be what you are to me

MAY I PASS

May I pass with your lips upon mine
Lips I've come to know divine
A final kiss to bid adieu
Your final act to say I love you

Know this with my final breath
As I embrace what we know death
That none have known a love more true
As the love I've felt for you

I have loved others, I confess
I loved them different though not less
But you stand apart from all the rest
Your love the object of my life's quest

When I'm to die, let me die in bliss
With my last breath, let me know your kiss

THANK YOU MY DEAREST

Thank you My Dearest
For saving my life
Accept my offer
Decreasing my strife

A simple yes
Is all I need hear
To make me happy
If your answer sincere

I've always known
You were the one
I need you as much
As life needs the sun

If you know not by now
How I feel for you
Then I'm at a loss
What to say and do

ARE YOU THERE

Are you there
Are you in my sphere
Can you feel the gravity
Can you feel what you mean to me

Do you understand the words I speak
Do you understand the love I seek
Do you realize what we could be
Do you realize the vision I see

I see you and I together as one
I see two become four before we're done
I have held you three in loving embrace
I have seen the approval upon your face

How I wish these dreams were reality
But these dreams remain dreams whilst dreamed but by me

WHERE ARE YOU, NOT WITH ME

Where are you, not with me
Not in the arms where you should be
Not with he to whom your love profess
Where are you, I can but guess

I await you, you don't appear
The concern is more than I can bear
Great worry I feel when you fail to show
I await you, where did you go

I'm a fool, that much is plain
In my heart I know I'll be a fool again
For I cannot deny the feelings I feel
I'm may be a fool, but my love is real

Loving you has been both Heaven and Hell
Loving you has been both blessing and spell

© John Patrick Boutilier, 2017, All Rights Reserved.

SWEET DREAMS

Sweet dreams
Wish you were here
Tight in my arms
Knowing passion sincere

You'd know no sleep
Were you in my embrace
For my want is strong
And there in your face

I see the passion that you feel
Is as intense as that I feel for you
A passion that is born of love
A passion born of love that's true

Oh how I wish that you were here
That we might share our love sincere

THE NUMBER OF LIES YOU DARE TO ME TELL

The number of lies you dare to me tell
Speaks well of what you truly feel for me
I refuse to buy all the lies you sell
The false hope you offer one day we'll be

There was a time when I dared to believe
But my naivety is now long past
I gave you my trust, you did but deceive
And therein our relationship was cast

I can at best offer to be your friend
Someone to provide you needed advice
A shoulder to lean on, I'm willing lend
If you promise to no longer entice

No more than that am I willing explore
Till sure you are willing offer me more

LOVE OF MY LIFE

Love of my life
She who gives life meaning
The reason for my being
My love
You

Love of my life
She who is my essence
The reason for my presence
The air I breathe
You

Love of my life
Though I've never known your embrace
I know there's none could replace
She I love
You

You are my reason for being
All the beauty I'm seeing
The one and only true
The love of my life
You

EVER ONE TO BE

Who?
You
Why?
Love
When?
Always
Where?
Everywhere
What?
Us

The answers are so simple
How can it be you cannot see
We were meant to be together
Ever one, you and be

I HAVE NEVER

I have never written anything I thought done
Tomorrow I might add more based on new experience
Upon reflection more insight might be gained

But right now
My words reflect this moment
How I feel in my heart

Fleeting as the words may seem
It is how I feel
This is me

The words I'm saying
They come from deep within my soul
Too often well beyond control

Because truth refuses be denied
I cannot hide what I feel inside
And what I feel inside is strong and true
What I feel inside is I love you

MY LOVE

Do you know what you are
Let me tell you
You are my everything
Every question I ask
Every answer I find
The one
My reason

Do you know who you are
Let me tell you
You are the cause for my being
The air that I breathe
The beat of my heart
My greatest desire
My love

IN THE DARKNESS I CAN SEE YOU

In the darkness I can see you
For you are my guiding light
In my choices, you I follow
For in you I see the right

In my day you are the sunshine
For it is you makes me warm
In times when others run for shelter
With you I'd weather any storm

In every moment of my life
For you I offer up my heart
May there never be a morning
When I awake with us apart

And may I never know a night
Without you in my arms, held tight

IF I WERE TO OFFER

If I were to offer you my heart
Would you promise not tear it apart
If my offer were a promise of love to be
Would you offer your love to me

If I promised my love would ever be true
A love given to none but you
Would you this vow be willing to swear
That you would for me ever be there

If I announced to the world that I loved you
Would this be something you too would do
If I spent my life loving only thee
What from you might I expect to see

Love me yes or love me no
I love you more than you'll ever know

IF I WERE TO SAY I LOVED YOU

If I were to say I loved you
Would you say you loved me too
Would you mean it the way I do
Would your words of love be true

If I said I'd leave you never
That I would love you well beyond forever
Would you believe my words sincere
Or would their truth escape your ear

If I held you every night
In my embrace so warm and tight
Would that alleviate your doubt
Would that your insecurity rout

There is only so much this man can do
To prove to you his love is true
But if you know something I do not know
Please inform that I might bestow

If I were to say I loved you
Would you say you loved me too
Would you mean it the way I do
Would your words of love be true

IF YOU DARE

If you dare have as much faith in yourself
As the faith I feel in my heart for you
You will then understand my confidence
I know you'll accomplish what you need do

You are so much stronger than you believe
Many times have I admired your deeds
You do what you do, you do it with ease
You achieve your goals with minimum needs

Do not let doubts undermine who you are
You are the example, you're the ideal
A guiding light in a world of darkness
A genuine heart where so few are real

You accept the pain, so accept the joy
You've got all the skills, you need but employ

TAKE MY HAND

Take my hand
Let me show you the way
Not that I know the path
Only that I want you with me

We may wander aimlessly in the night
At least that is how it may seem to be
But I know together we'll ever move forward
We'll find the light, you and me

I love you, I always have
I love you, right or wrong
I love you, I always will
I love you, my love is strong

My love is strong enough to weather the greatest storm
However cold the world may be, our love shall keep us warm

WERE YOU BUT HERE TO KISS AND HOLD

Were you but here to kiss and hold
What other wonders might be told
What tales in the morning might we tell
What might we quiet, what might we yell

I would scream and shout the joy I knew
Though never would I give name to you
Not because of fear or shame
But to lovingly protect your name

But if you want to tell of me
I give you permission to let it be
Scream to all that I love you
If that is what you choose to do

I am right in she I've made my choice
Let it be known that I rejoice

I WANT YOU TO SEE SOMETHING BEAUTIFUL

I want you to see something beautiful
It is everywhere in your life
But you need to do one thing to see it
Open your eyes

Look in the mirror
Do you see what I see
What is more beautiful than that image
Nothing

Every hair, every line
Every blemish, every scar
By nature was made to define you
You are among billions unique

Appreciate yourself
Your beauty
Both within and without
Then you will better appreciate the beauty in everyone else

Beauty lies in the eyes of the beholder, yes
So does ugliness
See with an eye for beauty in all
And you will never see ugliness again

I DON'T BELIEVE WORDS

I don't believe words
Matters not the words you say
Your deeds define you
If my love is what you yearn
'Tis by deeds my heart you'll earn

Lies pass the lips so easy
Ears grow deaf to spoken truth
I've now long been deaf
'Tis result of those deceive
We cannot believe

'Tis not your blame, nor is it mine
Bad experience is the fault
Could I remove it from my soul I would
But I've not yet healed from its assault

ALL IN MY WORLD

My arms are wanting of your presence
Ever needing your embrace
Without you here within my arms
All in my world seems out of place

My eyes are wanting of your beauty
'Tis sight of you brings light to day
Without you here there is no colour
All in my world seems cold and grey

My heart is wanting of your love
For you're the reason that it beats
Without you here I but exist
All deeds in life seem useless feats

I'm but a fragment of who I should be
Without you here to make whole of me

I AM THE ONE WHO LOVES YOU

I am the one who loves you
However much you might deny
There is no one in this entire world
Who loves you more than I

I am blind to your imperfections
That which others deem to be
To me you couldn't be more perfect
The perfect girl for me

Have you ever felt incomplete
Like a part of you was missing
I've felt incomplete so many years
Like a singer absent voice for singing

In our very first kiss I knew it was you
She I had wanted my entire life through

SUCH BEAUTY

Such beauty I see in she I see
That I think the term beauty was defined by she
My words speak truth, they're not empty dear
I said what I said and what I said was sincere

No beauty compares to the beauty that be
To the beauty of she who stands before me
I know it will come of no surprise
That I am seduced by your beautiful eyes

What lies behind those eyes I see
Those eyes that have so captured me
What is it in those eyes so takes control
Over my heart and over my soul

I admit I know not but I am willing learn more
If you are but willing allow me explore

ONE DOES NOT NEED PERFECT GRAMMAR FOR POETRY

One does not need perfect grammar for poetry.
One needs but be able convey an idea, a thought, a feeling.
Say what you want to say as if none but you were listening.
If you are true unto yourself
There, in those words, may lie a poem.

ATTACKS ON FREE SPEECH

Attacks on free speech are not only attacks on freedom
They are attacks on intelligence
They are attacks on art

Political correctness is an attack on free speech
It is an attack on constructive discourse
It is an attack on truth

Rigged elections are an attack on freedom of choice
They are attacks on democracy
They are attacks on representation

Denying sexual orientation is more than just an attack on freedom
It is an attack on nature
It is an attack on love

Attacks on free speech are attacks against our children
They're attacks against me
They're attacks against you

Free speech is both a right and a duty
You have the right to speak your mind
You have the duty to think before you speak

Free speech is not a license to hate
It is a license to voice an opinion
It is a license to present a point of view

Freedom of speech is worth fighting for
It is worth dying for
It is worth living for

EVIL DOES EXIST

Evil does exist
But then again so does good
Make the proper choices
Do the things you know you should

Try to never hurt another
Be it by voice or be it by deed
But accept the fact there will be times
When such actions are the need

We must stand and fight for the weak
When evil threatens their life and limb
When evil threatens their rights and freedom
When evil threatens their light to dim

Evil does exist
And it our duty to fight it wherever seen
With every fiber of our being
Till from all evil our lives are clean

OUR JOB

It is our job to tell the government what to do
They represent the people
Stop searching a benevolent tyrant
A shepherd for the sheeple

If you accept the pablum they offer you
Swallow their act and their lies
Then you alone must bear the blame
When you they victimize

You do not belong to them
You're not their resource to be used
You weren't born to be their slave
You don't exist to be abused

You are free men and women
Each and every one deserving respect
As to all the starving and homeless
Not one deserves such neglect

Yet politicians cut support for the poor
While increasing their own wages
Using your money to feast like kings
Have sex with underage pages

Their legacy is theirs to choose
But such is true of us as well
Do we continue to serve the beast
Or send the beast back to hell

IF AMERICA FAILS

If America fails, democracy fails
Put the bankers in jail
Follow Iceland's example
Give none the guilty bail

Say no established dollar
The central bank currency
Create an honest dollar
Create a new economy

Say no to the Bilderbergs
Say no to the liars and thieves
Say no to those who seek control
Say no to those who deceive

Take control from the criminals in power
Put them in the darkest cell
Those who preyed upon our children
Introduce them to the darkest hell

DELETE AND BLOCK

Delete and block any poetry site
Who dares hide the poems we post
For they are what the creative mind
Like you and I detest most
Publish their deeds on your sites
Let every poet know
So these sites will disappear
And the better sites will grow
I will tolerate no Nazi
Nor allow my work be censored
What I write is from the heart
Not for an ignorant bastard
And I know I speak for every poet
For we are of one kind
We speak the truth as best we can
And we are of free mind
Though the message sent may differ
And we may not agree
You have the right to post your view
If you give the same to me
And if you deny me the right
To say what I have to say
I will do my best to silence you
Show all your Nazi way
It's easy to stop a Fascist
Speak up in early hour
Nip the weed in the bud
Before it gains too much power
And where they think they're in full bloom
Not needing fear you or I
Expose them all for who they are
And they will go goodbye
There is no darkness wants the light

For in the light truth is revealed
The darkness thus succumbs to truth
Therein their fate is sealed

FALSE GODS AND FALSE BELIEVERS

The people are responsible for destroying gods
Especially the false ones
Those who by their wealth or position
Assume they are more than fools
It is not your right to dispose of them
It is a divine decree

No god demands worship
Worship is a demand of the weak
God is not weak
God is not cruel nor is God vindictive
God is a parent
And God forgives of all children, everything
Anyone who says other of God is a liar and represents Satan

If you do not accept your brothers and sisters
Whatever their nature
Then it is you who are damned
Hate damns you
Love saves

Some condemn those gay and lesbian
Do you not see the beauty
Such slows the growth of the species
Also it provide parents for orphans
A divine solution is it not

Those who most think themselves holy
Are usually the furthest from the lord
Pride and misunderstanding blinds
Leads them fall into the pit
Where most of them belong

Love and you will be saved
Hate and you will perish
Set aside your prejudice and live
For we all are one
Save those who chose not see the truth
The damned

TO CHANGE THE WORLD

To change the world we must teach our children to read
As we teach them to read we must teach them to discern
They must be taught to differentiate propaganda from fact
And when such is needed turn knowledge to act

A patriot represents the people first
The soldier owes more to the citizen than the general
When the government is willing turn you against your brother
How long will it be till the enemy's your mother

© John Patrick Boutilier, 2017, All Rights Reserved.

THE HARDEST THING TO BELIEVE

Sometimes the truth is the hardest thing to believe
Most likely because it's true
And who wants to believe that

© John Patrick Boutilier, 2017, All Rights Reserved.

I WISH LOVE AND PEACE WERE GENETIC

I wish love and peace were genetic
I'd encourage the peaceful to foster many children
But it isn't
Thus we must rely on example and education
Imperfect as it is

A VISION

One thing you can count on
Where there are rich who seek absolute power
Eventually they will destroy each other
Each seeking dominance over the others

It's their nature to destroy
To ruin all that is good
For as all human parasites regarding resources
They seek complete control

There's no loyalty amongst the mad
And when we, the meek, think it's our darkest hour
'Tis in their greed will lie our victory
'Tis from their greed will shine our freedom

For in their greed lies their weakness
While in our sharing lies our strength
'Tis in their greed they stand alone
While we who share are abundant

There's more than enough for all
If our greed we set aside
We all could live in Eden
If we'd choose but to share

ALL PEOPLE ARE ONE

All people are one
All descend from Africa
Brothers and sisters

TWO THINGS ARE ABSOLUTE

Two things absolute
Life and its opposite death
Make your life matter

Find someone to love
Love them with all of your heart
Always treat them well

Be an example
Show compassion and respect
Try to cause no harm

TREAT ALL AS EQUAL

Treat all as equal
Though you receive not the same
Respect therein earned

LET'S ROAR

Everything great that has ever been done has started with one
person who stood up and made change happen.
Imagine what we can do working together.
There is a choice to be made.
You can be the lion or you can be the sheep.
I say let's roar.

FOR JFK, MLK JR AND RFK

I do not hide, I declare
I do not descend, I ascend
I do not retreat, I defeat
In truth, I owe my strength
For even in my absence it will bear witness
In time all truth will be known
And the guilty exposed
I did not die to disappear
My death had purpose
And my memory will linger on
Until all have what they deserve
Until every man, woman and child
Whatever their colour
Whatever their religion
Whatever their status knows this
Freedom

YOU'RE NOT BUT A FRAUD

You need so little but you want so much
You say you're grounded but you're out of touch
You think you're a sage but we know you're a fool
You claim to be benevolent but we know you're cruel

Who do you think you are
You're not a star
Not a star by far
Though you fancy yourself a god
You're not to be awed
You're not but a fraud

You consider you our better but we know you are naught
You claim that you're perfect but with flaws you've been caught
You think you are the highest but we know how low you go
You think you have the answers but there's nothing that you know

In time the truth I know you'll see
Coming from those like me
Who will remain free
Though you fancy yourself the master
Every push pushes faster
The moment of your disaster

You consider yourself important but you're just a parasite
You think you've earned your way but you've stolen day and night
You say you believe in freedom but by your actions you enslave
You see yourself as knight but you're the darkest type of knave

The world is ours to share
If you dare to be fair
You too can care
There's more than enough for everyone

Let the greed be done
All avarice shun

THE TRUTH

Truth is not a matter of belief
Believe or not it is what it is
It exists beyond the arrogant human mind
Truth is fact

Truth does not evolve
Our understanding does
Knowledge is an ever increasing resource
It brings us nearer the real

Dogma is death to learning
It is a synonym for ignorance
For in our supposition we know anything
We lose our ability to learn

Keep your mind open
Maintain a sharp intellect
Use logic and data to guide
But never assume you know

I AM NOT PC

I am not PC
I am real
I will tell you the truth
Tell you what I feel

And if you're offended
Know I don't care
I speak the truth
With facts I'm aware

If I consider you evil
I am bound to offend
For I am against you
Beginning to end

But if you are good
You have nothing to fear
And when you're attacked
In defense I'll be there

Words are weapons
That much is true
But the truth is a danger
To only a few

To the pure of heart
The truth is benign
But to the evil
It is wrath divine

TYRANTS ARE MORTAL

Tyrants are mortal
Their flesh as weak as their minds
They can be removed

Fear not these bullies
For all bullies are cowards
Bring them to their knees

Freedom is not free
It often comes at great cost
Will you sacrifice

Dying for freedom
Is both honour and duty
Live beyond yourself

SOMETIMES WHEN I DREAM

Sometimes when I dream
I live the life I thought I'd live
I'm with the perfect woman
I have the perfect job
I live in the perfect home

Then I awake to reality
Where I am alone
I hate what I do
I live in the humblest of abodes
And prospects dwindle

The disappointment is severe
The stains on my pillow bear witness
But I will not give up the dream
Nor the hope of making it real
Too much has already been invested

I believe dreams can come true
Despite all evidence to the contrary
I know it's happened for some
I just need to make it happen for me
Choose the proper course

As long as I have strength to draw a breath
I will continue to pursue my dreams
And I will act to make them real
Till I can act no more
Or I have achieved my goals

BE A SLAVE TO NONE AND A MASTER TO AS MANY

Be a slave to none and a master to as many
Though we differ in knowledge, in belief and in skill
We differ not in our rights
In justice we are the same

The strong are meant to protect the weak
The wealthy to provide for the poor
The knowing to enlighten the naive
The free to unshackle the slave

Rise to your responsibility
Take pride in your role
You were given gifts and advantages
Use them for the greatest purpose

Where there is want of money
If you are able, provide
Where there is want of knowledge
If you are able, teach

Where there is want of peace
Denounce war
Where there is want of hope
Hold out your hand

There is no greater power than you
How will you use your strength
Will you be benevolent
Will you rise to your potential

WE CAN ONLY ACHIEVE IF WE ATTEMPT

We can only achieve if we attempt
We may fail
We may succeed
In trying alone a battle has been won

But if we attempt not
If we fail to rise against wrong
If we bury our heads in the sand and we do nothing
We lose

In such a case we have surrendered without a fight
That is true failure
The true and the righteous stand for their principles
In that alone they find victory

Through the message
The right can defy both defeat and death
For unlike the messenger
The message is immortal

I JUST THOUGHT I'D ASK

Why injure when you can heal
Why scold when you can teach
Why lie when you can tell the truth
Why be less when you can be so much more

Why death when there is life
Why despair when there is hope
Why fight when there is cooperation
Why cry when you could smile

Perhaps I'm just a simpleton
Because I simply don't understand
It makes no sense at all to me
And thus I query why

Answer not if you've neither time nor care
I just thought I'd ask

I HAVE SEEN

I have seen the face of the beast
And I have learned its name
It is an evil, sick, demented
Product of a mind insane

I have seen the battle come
And been shown how it ends
The evil are eliminated
When the light of truth descends

Martyrs they made lead the way
In the conquest of the lie
There will be no mercy shown
When the evil are brought to die

That which it had offered
Is that it will receive
Such justice will be given those
In the evil chose believe

And what I hold in my hand
Is more than just a sword
It represents my faith and love
In Jesus, the true Lord

DISAGREEMENT IS NOT HATE

Disagreement is not hate
Disagreement is not intolerance
Disagreement is an exercise of the intelligent mind
Only evil fears intelligence

The louder you complain
The clearer your evil nature is seen
For only evil fears be questioned
Only evil fears the truth

Oh please do complain
And oh please do be loud
So all the world will see true you
So what you seek be not allowed

I will not be denied my speech
And where all else may be silent
I will scream truth back at you
For such is what I'm born to do

I will not tolerate your lies
And I am not alone
Evil may be legion
But the light will soon be shown

DENIAL IS INACTION

Denial is inaction
Inaction is submission
Submission is slavery
Slavery is worse than death

We would rather die free
Than ever for a moment a slave to be
Know this you tyrannical monstrosity
The one to bow will be you not we

Force is an evil
Evil is a lie
A lie is a weapon
A weapon is a tool of war

If I am forced into a fight
Be it day or be it night
We will fight with all our might
And on our side we hold the right

Right is freedom
Freedom is peace
Peace is love
Love is God

AN EDUCATION OF LIES

An education of lies is the blame of the teacher
Be they a parent, the government or a preacher
And where the child is taught to hate
The teacher is blame for the child's fate

WE ARE ONE

To be forced into violence
To be forced to kill and injure
Even though in self defense
Injures the soul of all
Why not love
Why not live in peace
Abandon that which angers
Embrace each other
Love each other
We are one
All are brothers
All are sisters
Anything that divides our family
Is a lie
It is an evil
Call it what you will
Be it colour: a trick of light
Be it religion: superstition
Be it politics: lust for power
Be it greed or be it envy
It is all a lie
The truth
You and I
We are one

LESS THAN A MAN

I am a loving man
I could never condemn my children to eternal suffering
I am compassionate and forgiving

I am an honest man
I fear neither question nor doubt
I am what I am and that is but a man

Surely God is more forgiving
Surely God is more compassionate
Surely God does not fear the truth

I love
I desire peace
I want all to be one

Surely God wants peace
Surely God wants love
Surely God is a better being than I

If not
It is not a god at all
It is, if fact, less than a man

I'VE BEEN THINKING

I've been thinking thoughts
Thoughts I never thought I'd think
Thoughts that keep me awake at night
Thoughts that put me on the brink

Liberty has been attacked
Attacked by actions of the beast
Attacked so deep it bruised the core
Attacked by that which must be ceased

This vile cancer must be removed
Removed from every living cell
Removed for the good of everyone
Removed and sent back to hell

The time is here to make our stand
Stand against the Devil's legions
Stand and fight for love and peace
Stand and fight in all Earth's regions

The evil cannot be allowed to live
Live to spread both death and hate
Live to enslave and deny truth voice
Live to torture and discriminate

I have these thoughts because I see
I see both right and good disappear
I see evil spread worldwide unchecked
I see its influence everywhere

I have these thoughts because I'm a man
A man for whom the truth is a prize
A man who champions peace and love
A man who sees through all their lies

WHEN I WAS A SHORTER MAN

When I was a shorter man
I wasn't quite as tall
Now that I'm a taller man
Does that mean I'm not as small

Seems the definition
Has changed a bit with time
Tall no longer means more high
I've seen it mean neck deep in slime

I want to be a higher man
Height means not to me
A man a thousand feet more tall
Could a lesser man be

'Tis not money nor possessions
For such men oft seem so sad
'Tis not power nor adulation
For such men oft seem so bad

What is it then makes a man
What makes him stand above
I have learned it is compassion
And his ability to love

You must be strong for the weak
You must be guide for those lost
You must be provider for the needy
You must be there despite the cost

You must be a light in the darkness
You must be a shield against the sword
You must be a friend to those abandoned

You must be both truth and reward

When I was a shorter man
There was much I didn't know
But I try my best everyday
By His example grow

ANYTHING THAT DIVIDES A PEOPLE

Anything that divides a people is evil
Good only brings us together
The human race is one people
Evil is that which cuts the tether

Be it colour
Be it religion
Be it politics
It is evil if it creates division

Be it height
Be it weight
Be it intelligence
There's no debate

We are one
What divides is a lie
It is time to see the truth
To every lie say goodbye

If you are taught to hate
You have been mislead
Hate not your brothers and your sisters
Fill your heart with love instead

Anything that divides a people is evil
In your heart you know that's true
We can change the world for the better
The change, Dear sibling, begins with you

BETWEEN YOU AND I

I love
You hate
I want to bring together
You want to separate

I want peace
You want war
I want that we share
You want more

I want equality
You want to dominate
I want to live as one
You want to devastate

I want Heaven
You want Hell
I want to share the truth
You have none to tell

RISE OR FALL

Love and hate are not the same
They are as opposite as life and death
They are the heartbeat or the heartbeat not
They are the presence or lack of breath

I breathe so I live
I live so I must care
I care for I am part
I am part of what is here

What is here displeases me
For all I see and hear are lies
Everything I am presented
More there's some I seem despise

But there is a light
A light of hope, however weak
A light that may bring us peace
A light towards the truth we seek

One day, I hope, the truth we'll know
Love is what will save us all
Love not and we are doomed to die
We must choose to rise or fall

PEACEFUL COEXISTANCE

"Peaceful coexistence requires a commitment to that goal alone and the abandonment of any belief that would hinder its manifestation.
It is unfortunate that so many claim the desire for peace while clinging to racial and religious divides.
What is race is to the blind?
It is nothing more than a meaningless concept.
Its continued propagation due to those with working eyes but lack of sight.
What is religion to the blind?
A fate far worse than blindness of the eyes.
For too oft religion blinds the mind even of those with sight."

© John Patrick Boutilier, 2017, All Rights Reserved.

IF WE ARE SILENCED

If we are silenced
Our existence means nothing
Without a voice
We are but parts in a machine
Parts easily replaced
Parts lacking value
Cheap and expendable
Like a redundant screw

ONE

One
An imperative
If peace is to exist
We must all be part of

One
A desire of the just
A fear of the greedy
A commitment to trust

One
The truth in a word
What we all are
Though some think it absurd

One
There are no races
We are all human
With slightly variant faces

One
All else is a lie
If we fail to embrace
How many will die

One
That is what I see
I see me when I look at you
What do you see when you look at me

BETRAYAL

There is no worse betrayal
Than the betrayal of a friend
And such betrayal is even worse
From one thought loyal till the end

Ask Caesar how he felt
When stabbed deepest by the knife
Of Brutus whom he loved as son
And loved for all his life

It seems so often those held dear
Those in whom we place greatest trust
Are those whom we must most beware
Having knife in hand, ready to thrust

If you must bury your knife
Then I bid you bury it deep
At least betray me with some mercy
When you send me to my sleep

IF YOU FEEL ALONE

If you feel alone
Not sure what to do
Know this sincere
I am there with you

Fear no evil
For you are the right
There is no darkness
Can deny your light

When brought you pain
From evil hand
Find you comfort
In where you stand

Right and love
Both powers great
Embrace them both
They are not prate

You are the lead
You are the way
You are the future
The brighter day

With your love
Our thoughts align
But through compassion
You prove yourself mine

YOU HAVE THE OPTION

When you invite someone into your home
And they begin to destroy all you value
Do you idly sit back and watch
Or do you do what you know you have to

I am a man of peace
But I know there are times for war
Come into my home and tell me how to live
I will drive you from my shore

Rape my women and my children
I will see to it you die
I'll show to you the same mercy
That you would show to I

None, none
We know what must be done
If anyone must be eliminated
We know you are the one

None, none
Arm everyone with guns
We will resist your attack
You'll be none when we are done

Give up the lie you have been told
For you have been mislead
You have the option war and hate
Or peace and love instead

None, none
None left when we are done
Just as you would have with us
You'll be none when we are done

I DESIRE NOTHIING MORE

I desire nothing more
Than all humanity to be as one
But as long as we believe in gods
My desire will not be done

How ignorant is the mind
In that a god believe
How can a mind cling to the lie
That a divine being be

Do we know not of science
Not know of cause and effect
Can't we with all that we have learned
In god just reject

God remains an opiate
A chain disguised as hug
Meant to enslave the believer
God is but a drug

All the enslaved masses
With religion in their heads
High on their opiate
Are akin the living dead

THE TREE

We see from our place
Here in the tree
What you witness day by day
May be different to me

I see the left
But you saw the right
I see the day
But you see the night

Neither is wrong
Is but point of view
What is obvious to me
May be obscure to you

But I know this
We both inhabit the tree
Despite our perspective
You're the same as me

Can you offer me the love
I can offer to you
That this tree may prosper
Its leaves ever new

The tree is humanity
Its branches abound
They grow ever apart
Though they grow from same ground

We share the same water
We share the same soil
We share the same air

We share the same toil

We are all seeking light
Wherever our place
A ray of hope
To find our space

We are a tree
One under the sun
We must work together
That the tree ever live on

I THINK

I think
And therefore I am a threat
Think
And be a threat with me

Be a voice of truth
Be a voice of opposition
Be a voice of change
Be a voice of vision

Be a voice of love
Be a voice of brotherhood
Be a voice of freedom
Be a voice of good

Be a voice of peace
Say no to war and hate
Be what you were meant to be
Do it now before too late

ONLY THE FRIGHTENED

Only the frightened seek to inspire fear
Only the weak seek to dominate
Only a lie fears to be questioned
Only a fool fears to debate

The courageous lead by example
The strong support the weak
The right welcomes to be questioned
The sage gives all a chance to speak

If you have no answer
Then of course you fear a why
If you fear any question at all
Then what you say must be a lie

Only a lie fears the truth
Only the wrong fears the right
Only evil fears the good
Only the dark fears the light

A WOMAN

A woman
She is to be prized
Her very many special gifts
A joy be realized

The tenderness of her caress
The welcome in her smile
The healing comes from her embrace
So relieves a man from trial

What tragedy she cannot fix
With but a loving glance
There is no pain she cannot soothe
With her eyes entrance

I say this now
And believe it true
Treat a woman wrong
Wrong will visit you

WE

We are the light
We are the right
We will defeat the darkness
We will defeat the night

We are the true
We are the few
We will overcome the numbers
We will overcome you

We are the real
We are the ideal
We will eliminate the hate
We will eliminate your zeal

We are the way
We are the brighter day
We will bring both love and peace
We will bring all war to cease

For we are the light
We are the right
We will defeat the darkness
We will defeat the night

HELP YOUR FELLOW HUMAN AND YOU ARE BLESSED

Help your fellow human and you are blessed
Ignore their need and you are cursed
All humans are one under the sun
It is our duty do what need be done

Feed the hungry with food you can spare
Clothe the naked with what you don't wear
Find shelter for those who live on the street
Give love and respect to all people you meet

Be wise for the fool
Be kind to the cruel
Be strong for the weak
Be sword for the meek

We need each other, but most we need you
We need you to see what is obviously true
Matters not what divides, nor wrong or right
Matters only you be a light in the night

Shine my friends
Shine and shine true
Shine for those in need
As others shine for you

IF YOU ARE NOT HELPING

If you are not helping
You are a hindrance
Be more than just a weight
Add your thoughts to the debate

And if you speak
Speak with knowledge
Waste not our time with mere belief
With our time be not a thief

We appreciate what comes from heart
But from the facts we can't depart
Sometimes beliefs we must let go
When the truth we want to know

I am open to all ideas
But for belief I demand the truth
If you want me in you believe
You must stay true and not deceive

For if you lie to me knowingly
If one statement you know untrue
I will doubt everything you say
My belief ever kept at bay

But show me the data and show me the true
And I will put my faith in you
Sometimes it's doubt we must let go
When the truth we come to know

FREE THE WOMEN

Free the women
They are not your equal
They are your better
No man exists without a mother
No man exists not wanting her love
What man could bear what the woman does
And still smile
And still prepare dinner
And still keep the home pristine

No man I have even known
Was as strong or was as brave
And I have known heroic men
When I see indignity put upon on her
When I see her subjugated
It fills my heart with rage
And I decry
And I wonder why
And then I realize

He who lessens a woman
Is weak among true men
In his deed he lessens self
He who enslaves a woman
Is not man enough to win a woman's love
For he is a nothing
And a nothing is powerless
And a nothing is unworthy
And a nothing is what you are

Free the women
In doing so you will free yourself
You will free yourself from the lie

A man cannot take a woman
Sex is not the love he craves
Rape but proves a man an animal
It marks him the lowest of the low
It marks him impotent and weak
It marks him a disease to be eliminated

SPEAK THE TRUTH

Speak the truth
Or speak not at all
Gain my ear
Or build a wall

A single lie
Makes you a liar
A deceiver
Fuel for the fire

Speak the truth
And have my respect
Honour is something
I cannot neglect

A man who stands for his beliefs
However wrong I believe them be
If in his heart he believes them true
How different is this man from me

Speak the truth
Or speak not at all
Gain my ear
Or build a wall

GRANNY'S GOT A GUN

Granny's got a gun
And it's loaded
And she's ready to fight
She's devoted
She's given her life
To the red, white and blue
She'll defend the constitution
She'll defend you
Granny's got a gun
Granny's got a gun

Granny's got a gun
And she'll use it
If that's the option you provide
She'll choose it
She's never missed once
Not once in her life
She's as accurate as Roger Stone
With political advice
Granny's got a gun
Granny's got a gun

She's the only person in this world Putin truly fears
The elite have been afraid of her for nearly 90 years
But no one's ever tried approach
They simply wouldn't dare

Granny's got a gun
And she's true
She has nothing to hide
From me and you
She states it as she sees it
And never once been wrong

She says that war is coming
'Twill be here before too long
Granny's got a gun
Granny's got a gun

Granny is everything to me
She is such a sage
And she's been teaching me to shoot
Ever since I came of age
She has been around so long
Some claim the world is hers
And she's not embarrassed to show you
Her many woolly mammoth furs
Granny's got a gun
Granny's got a gun

She trains the green berets
She trains the navy seals
Her hand to hand is second to none
Granny does what she feels

She's the only person in this world Putin truly fears
The elite have been afraid of her for nearly 90 years
But no one's ever tried approach
They simply wouldn't dare

Granny's got a gun
And it's loaded
And she's ready to fight
She's devoted
She's given her life
To the red, white and blue
She'll defend the constitution
She'll defend you
Granny's got a gun
Granny's got a gun

Granny's got a gun
Granny's got a gun

YOU CREATE

You create your reality
Act and you can make it your vision
Act not, then succumb to the reality of others
And know the consequences of sloth
Of ignorance
Of apathy
Of stupidity

Your world is what you will have it
If you are prepared to make a stand
Stand up for what you believe
Stand up and oppose the evil
The liars
The deceivers
The believers

You have the power to create Heaven
But you must choose to do so
The burden of this noble goal
Lies upon both I and you
The good
The right
The seers of the light

We can create a world of peace
Where all people share and cooperate
But before this can be manifest
We must desire be a reality
One people
One goal
One purpose

GIVE LOVE TO ME

Give love to me
I will give love to you
Be my enemy
I will be death to you

Be savage and cruel
Treat mine unwell
Then yours will beg
To know the horrors of hell

Student of Caesar
As I have been
I know the ways of war
I know how to win

You will submit
For such is your name
Mine is the might
Yours is the lame

Escape the lie
Accept the true
Forsake the evil
It seeks to make you

All are one
That is reality
Let us banish all
Prevents it from be

SOCIAL "BULLSHIT" WARRIORS

If I offend you
You deserve it
If I make you cry
Give growing up a try
I will not be bullied by you
Shove your PC up your ass
I will speak my mind
My words nice or unkind
You see there is this thing
Long been known as truth
If you don't want to hear it
If you are so afraid be near it
Then shut the fuck up and stay in your shell
Or do us a favour and go to hell

I AM NOT A MARTYR

I am not a martyr
Martyrs die
I am a warrior
I eliminate my enemy

Whoever you are
Whatever you be
Mine is the last smile
You will ever see

Yes, my smile
I will rejoice in your death
My purpose made clear
See you draw no breath

I am not a martyr
There is purpose to my life
Eliminate the enemy
Bring light to the night

WAKE UP

You cannot reason with the unreasonable
You cannot have peace with those who want war
You cannot inform those who will not listen
You cannot give enough to those who want more

You will have to fight for love
You will have to fight for peace
You will have to fight for freedom
You will have to fight for evil to cease

You cannot arm your enemy
You cannot accept the word of a liar
You cannot ever turn your back on them
You cannot believe them though you desire

You will have to fight for your child
You will have to fight for your friend
You will have to fight for yourself
You will have to fight or good will end

Open your eyes and see the true
It is either evil triumphs or it is you

THOUGH THE FLESH BE WEAK

Though the flesh be weak
There's no goal can't be achieved
If the will is strong

You'll find what you seek
The rewards you want received
Though journey be long

THE END

CPSIA information can be obtained
at www.ICGtesting.com
Printed in the USA
FSHW020952311219
65620FS

9 781542 534802